Presented to	From	Date
_____	_____	_____
_____	_____	_____
_____	_____	_____
_____	_____	_____
_____	_____	_____

♫ Alle Jahre wieder kommt das Christuskind
auf die Erde nieder wo wir Menschen sind ♫

♫ Every year again the Child Jesus comes
down upon this earth where we humans live ♫
— Alle Jahre wieder (Every year again)
by Johann Wilhelm Hey, 1837

A King James Christmas

Biblical Selections with Illustrations from Around the World

Edited by

Catherine Schuon

and

Michael Oren Fitzgerald

✦Wisdom Tales✦

Design by Susana Marín

Frontispiece and Cover: *The Virgin of the Sleigh*, Catherine Schuon, 1973
Title page: *Adoration of the Magi*, Fra Angelico, 1423–1424

Library of Congress Cataloging-in-Publication Data

A King James Christmas : Biblical selections with illustrations from around the world /
edited by Catherine Schuon and Michael Oren Fitzgerald.
    p. cm.
  Includes bibliographical references.
  ISBN 978-1-937786-03-8 (casebound : alk. paper) 1. Jesus Christ--Nativity--Juvenile
literature. 2. Christmas--Juvenile literature. 3. Jesus Christ--Teachings--Juvenile literature. I.
Schuon, Catherine, 1924- II. Fitzgerald, Michael Oren, 1949- III. Bible. N.T. Gospels. English.
Selections. 2012.
  BT315.A3 2012
  232.92--dc23
                                                                                                2012010726

Printed in China on acid-free paper
Production Date: June, 2012
Plant & Location: Printed by Everbest Printing (Guangzhou, China), Co. Ltd
Job / Batch: 105583

Wisdom Tales is an imprint of World Wisdom, Inc.

For information address Wisdom Tales,
P.O. Box 2682, Bloomington, Indiana 47402-2682

www.wisdomtalespress.com

Contents

Annunciation and Adoration of the Magi, Fra Angelico, before 1434

Preface

Some of my earliest and fondest childhood memories are of the time after Christmas Eve dinner when our family would gather together to listen as my parents, aunts, and uncles would each in turn read from a series of Gospel passages about the birth and childhood of Jesus Christ. It is not clear to me at what point I understood the meaning of each of the words; however, the annual narration, including our family discussions, left a powerful impression on me as a young child and each year I gained a better understanding—a learning process that continues to this day. The idea for this Christmas reader came as I was reflecting on these memories shortly after the birth of my first grandchild; I realized that we would soon be introducing another generation into our family tradition.

All Biblical selections are taken from the King James Version, completed in 1611, which is the most printed book in the history of the world. Forty-seven scholarly translators labored for almost eight years to create a work that represents a unique style which is neither the spoken nor written English of that day. Subsequent translations benefit from their work, yet no other translation surpasses this timeless classic in overall exactness combined with poetic eloquence.

Several features of this edition are designed to aid anyone who is reading it aloud, starting with the large font of the text. Because the passages follow the chronological events surrounding the birth of Christ, the reader does not have to move back and forth in the Bible by using book marks and written notations. The King James Version sometimes uses archaic words and expressions. Instead of presenting a glossary at the end of the book, more common expressions are given in brackets and in italics after certain words that may not be familiar to children. This allows the reader the option of pronouncing these synonyms in addition to, or instead of, the main text in order to create a more accessible experience for young listeners. Finally, the words of Christ are presented in red to make them more easily identifiable for the reader.

A King James Christmas is arranged into three distinct parts: I. The Birth of Christ; II. The Childhood of Christ; and III. The Teachings of Christ. The Biblical verses in Part I are the most often cited verses surrounding the birth of Christ. Part II presents the story of Jesus teaching in the temple at twelve years of age. There are many legends about his childhood that date back to the first centuries after his death, but this is the only canonical passage about that time of his life. Our family's Christmas Eve practice included the reading of this verse. Finally, in Part III, we listen to Jesus as he delivers his Sermon on the Mount, which is the first time The Lord's Prayer was spoken. This part allows parents to begin to answer to older children the inevitable question, "What did Jesus teach?" As in certain other editions of the King James Version, a number of section headers are included, which helpfully separate the different thoughts in The Sermon of the Mount for young readers. The three parts on the Birth, Childhood, and Teachings of Christ can be read altogether or in different combinations depending on the available time and on family circumstances.

"A work of art," as art historian Titus Burckhardt explains, "can without any mental effort on our part, convey to us immediately and 'existentially,' a particular intellectual truth or spiritual attitude, and thereby grant us all manner of insights...." Thus we have included illustrations to bring the canonical text to life for readers of all ages. Catherine Schuon has selected the works of art on these pages, which include re-productions of paintings, sculptures, illuminated manuscripts, and stained glass windows from across the globe and created over millennia. The book includes a number of Catherine Schuon's own paintings of the events surrounding the birth and life of Christ. These illustrations reflect the diversity of ways in which people of many nations have throughout history rendered homage to these holy events. Brief captions in the main text are supplemented with an Appendix that contains additional information about each work of art.

Our prayer is that these passages and works of art will provide spiritual nourishment for all who visit these pages and allow multiple generations to join together and commemorate the story of the birth of Jesus Christ.

Michael Fitzgerald
December, 2011
Bloomington, Indiana

Part I:

The Birth of Christ

These Biblical verses present the events surrounding the
birth of Christ in chronological order.

The Madonna of Humility, c. 1390, Lippo di Dalmasio

St. John the Baptist: Angel of the Desert, Russian icon, 7th century

Events Leading to the Birth of John the Baptist

Luke

1:5 There was in the days of Herod, the king of Judaea, a certain priest named Zacharias…: and his wife was … Elisabeth.

1:6 And they were both righteous before God, walking in all the commandments and ordinances of the Lord blameless.

1:7 And they had no child, because Elisabeth was barren, and they both were now well stricken [*advanced*] in years.

1:8 And it came to pass, that while he executed the priest's office before God in the order of his course,

1:9 According to the custom of the priest's office, his lot was to burn incense when he went into the temple of the Lord.

1:10 And the whole multitude of the people were praying without at the time of incense.

1:11 And there appeared unto him an angel of the Lord standing on the right side of the altar of incense.

1:12 And when Zacharias saw him, he was troubled, and fear fell upon him.

1:13 But the angel said unto him, "Fear not, Zacharias: for thy prayer is heard; and thy wife Elisabeth shall bear thee a son, and thou shalt call his name John.

1:14 And thou shalt have joy and gladness; and many shall rejoice at his birth.

1:15 For he shall be great in the sight of the Lord, and shall drink neither wine nor strong drink; and he shall be filled with the Holy Ghost [*Spirit*], even from his mother's womb.

1:16 And many of the children of Israel shall he turn unto the Lord their God.

1:17 And he shall go before him in the spirit and power of Elias, to turn the hearts of the fathers to the children, and the disobedient to the wisdom of the just; to make ready a people prepared for the Lord."

1:18 And Zacharias said unto the angel, "Whereby shall I know this? for I am an old man, and my wife well stricken [*advanced*] in years."

1:19 And the angel answering said unto him, "I am Gabriel, that stand in the presence of God; and am sent to speak unto thee, and to show thee these glad tidings.

1:20 And, behold, thou shalt be dumb [*silent*], and not able to speak, until the day that these things shall be performed, because thou believest not my words, which shall be fulfilled in their season."

1:21 And the people waited for Zacharias, and marveled that he tarried [*remained*] so long in the temple.

1:22 And when he came out, he could not speak unto them: and they perceived that he had seen a vision in the temple: for he beckoned [*signaled*] unto them, and remained speechless.

1:23 And it came to pass, that, as soon as the days of his ministration [*service*] were accomplished, he departed to his own house.

1:24 And after those days his wife Elisabeth conceived, and hid herself five months, saying,

1:25 "Thus hath the Lord dealt with me in the days wherein he looked upon me, to take away my reproach [*disgrace*] among men."

Opposite: The Naming of John, Fra Angelico, c. 1434–1435
Following pages: The Annunciation, Catherine Schuon, 1967

An Angel Visits Mary

Luke

1:26 And in the sixth month the angel Gabriel was sent from God unto a city of Galilee, named Nazareth,

1:27 To a virgin espoused [*betrothed*] to a man whose name was Joseph, of the house of David; and the virgin's name was Mary.

1:28 And the angel came in unto her, and said, "Hail, thou that art highly favored, the Lord is with thee: blessed art thou among women."

1:29 And when she saw him, she was troubled at his saying, and cast in her mind what manner of salutation this should be.

1:30 And the angel said unto her, "Fear not, Mary: for thou hast found favor with God.

1:31 And, behold, thou shalt conceive in thy womb, and bring forth a son, and shalt call his name JESUS.

1:32 He shall be great, and shall be called the Son of the Highest: and the Lord God shall give unto him the throne of his father David:

1:33 And he shall reign over the house of Jacob for ever; and of his kingdom there shall be no end."

1:34 Then Mary said unto the angel, "How shall this be, seeing I know not a man?"

1:35 And the angel answered and said unto her, "The Holy Ghost [*Spirit*] shall come upon thee, and the power of the Highest shall overshadow thee: therefore also that holy thing which shall be born of thee shall be called the Son of God.

Opposite: The Annunciation,
Catherine Schuon, 1967

1:36 And, behold, thy cousin Elisabeth, she hath also conceived a son in her old age; and this is the sixth month with her, who was called barren.

1:37 For with God nothing shall be impossible."

1:38 And Mary said, "Behold the handmaid [*servant*] of the Lord; be it unto me according to thy word." And the angel departed from her.

The Annunciation, Greek icon, early 14th century

The Annunciation, Fra Angelico, c. 1441

The Visitation,
Catherine
Schuon, 1970

The Visitation, Giotto, 1302–1305

The Holy Virgin Visits Elisabeth, Mother of John the Baptist

Luke

1:39 And Mary arose in those days, and went into the hill country with haste, into a city of Juda;

1:40 And entered into the house of Zacharias, and saluted Elisabeth.

1:41 And it came to pass, that, when Elisabeth heard the salutation of Mary, the babe leaped in her womb; and Elisabeth was filled with the Holy Ghost [*Spirit*]:

1:42 And she spake out with a loud voice, and said, "Blessed art thou among women, and blessed is the fruit of thy womb.

1:43 And whence is this granted to me, that the mother of my Lord should come to me?

1:44 For, lo, as soon as the voice of thy salutation sounded in mine ears, the babe leaped in my womb for joy.

The Visitation (detail), Fra Angelico, c. 1432–1434

1:45 And blessed is she that believed: for there shall be a performance [*fulfillment*] of those things which were told her from the Lord."

1:46 And Mary said, "My soul doth magnify the Lord,

1:47 And my spirit hath rejoiced in God my Savior.

1:48 For he hath regarded the low estate of his handmaid [*servant*]: for, behold, from henceforth all generations shall call me blessed.

1:49 For he that is mighty hath done to me great things; and holy is his name.

1:50 And his mercy is on them that fear him from generation to generation.

1:51 He hath showed strength with his arm; he hath scattered the proud in the imagination of their hearts.

1:52 He hath put down the mighty from their seats [*thrones*], and exalted them of low degree.

1:53 He hath filled the hungry with good things; and the rich he hath sent empty away.

1:54 He hath holpen [*helped*] his servant Israel, in remembrance of his mercy;

1:55 As he spake to our fathers, to Abraham, and to his seed for ever."

1:56 And Mary abode [*dwelled*] with her about three months, and returned to her own house.

The Magnificat, Catherine Schuon, 1969

"We bring you good tidings," detail from a painting by Catherine Schuon, 1971

The Angel Appears to Joseph, Husband of the Holy Virgin

Matthew

1:18 Now the birth of Jesus Christ was on this wise [*in this way*]: When as his mother Mary was espoused [*betrothed*] to Joseph, before they came together, she was found with child of the Holy Ghost [*Spirit*].

1:19 Then Joseph her husband, being a just man, and not willing to make her a public example, was minded to send her away privily [*secretly*].

1:20 But while he thought on these things, behold, an angel of the LORD appeared unto him in a dream, saying, "Joseph, thou son of David, fear not to take unto thee Mary thy wife: for that which is conceived in her is of the Holy Ghost [*Spirit*].

1:21 And she shall bring forth a son, and thou shalt call his name JESUS: for he shall save his people from their sins."

1:22 Now all this was done, that it might be fulfilled which was spoken of the Lord by the prophet, saying,

1:23 "Behold, a virgin shall be with child, and shall bring forth a son, and they shall call his name Emmanuel," which being interpreted is, "God with us."

1:24 Then Joseph being raised from his sleep, did as the angel of the Lord had bidden [*commanded*] him, and took unto him his wife:

1:25 And knew her not till she had brought forth her firstborn son: and he called his name JESUS.

The Angel Tells Joseph to Flee to Egypt, Church of St. Martin in Zillis, Switzerland, 1130

The Nativity, Alesso Baldovinetti, Fra Angelico, and assistants, c. 1441

The Birth of Christ

Luke

2:1 And it came to pass in those days, that there went out a decree from Caesar Augustus that all the world should be taxed....

2:3 And all went to be taxed, every one into his own city.

2:4 And Joseph also went up from Galilee, out of the city of Nazareth, into Judaea, unto the city of David, which is called Bethlehem; (because he was of the house and lineage of David:)

2:5 To be taxed with Mary his espoused [*betrothed*] wife, being great with child.

2:6 And so it was, that, while they were there, the days were accomplished that she should be delivered.

2:7 And she brought forth her firstborn son, and wrapped him in swaddling clothes, and laid him in a manger; because there was no room for them in the inn.

The Nativity, c. 1200

Annunciation to the Shepherds, School of Reichenau, early 11th century

2:8 And there were in the same country shepherds abiding in the field, keeping watch over their flock by night.

2:9 And, lo, the angel of the Lord came upon them, and the glory of the Lord shone round about them: and they were sore afraid.

2:10 And the angel said unto them, "Fear not: for, behold, I bring you good tidings of great joy, which shall be to all people.

2:11 For unto you is born this day in the city of David a Savior, who is Christ the Lord.

2:12 And this shall be a sign unto you; Ye shall find the babe wrapped in swaddling clothes, lying in a manger."

2:13 And suddenly there was with the angel a multitude of the heavenly host praising God, and saying,

2:14 "Glory to God in the highest, and on earth peace, good will toward men."

2:15 And it came to pass, as the angels were gone away from them into heaven, the shepherds said one to another, "Let us now go even unto Bethlehem, and see this thing which is come to pass, which the Lord hath made known unto us."

The Annunciation to the Shepherds,
Church of St. Martin in Zillis, Switzerland, 1130

The Annunciation to the Shepherds, fresco by Giotto, c. 1310

2:16 And they came with haste, and found Mary, and Joseph, and the babe lying in the manger.

2:17 And when they had seen it, they made known abroad the saying which was told them concerning this child.

2:18 And all they that heard it wondered at those things which were told them by the shepherds.

2:19 But Mary kept all these things, and pondered them in her heart.

2:20 And the shepherds returned, glorifying and praising God for all the things that they had heard and seen, as it was told unto them.

2:21 And when eight days were accomplished for the circumcising of the child, his name was called JESUS, which was so named of [*by*] the angel before he was conceived in the womb.

The Nativity, medieval illumination, France, 15th century

The Virgin of the Rose Garden, Stefan Lochner, c. 1448

The Nativity, Lou Houng-Nien, early 20th century

The Virgin and the Child, Lou Houng-Nien, early 20th century

The Adoration of the Three Kings

Matthew

2:1 Now when Jesus was born in Bethlehem of Judaea in the days of Herod the king, behold, there came wise men from the east to Jerusalem,

2:2 Saying, "Where is he that is born King of the Jews? for we have seen his star in the east, and are come to worship him."

2:3 When Herod the king heard these things, he was troubled, and all Jerusalem with him.

2:4 And when he had gathered all the chief priests and scribes of the people together, he demanded of them where Christ should be born.

2:5 And they said unto him, "In Bethlehem of Judaea: for thus it is written by the prophet,

2:6 'And thou Bethlehem, in the land of Juda, art not the least among the princes of Juda: for out of thee shall come a Governor, that shall rule my people Israel.'"

2:7 Then Herod, when he had privily [*secretly*] called the wise men, enquired of them diligently what time the star appeared.

2:8 And he sent them to Bethlehem, and said, "Go and search diligently for the young child; and when ye have found him, bring me word again, that I may come and worship him also."

Opposite: The Adoration of the Magi,
Catherine Schuon, 1968

2:9 When they had heard the king, they departed; and, lo, the star, which they saw in the east, went before them, till it came and stood over where the young child was.

2:10 When they saw the star, they rejoiced with exceeding great joy.

2:11 And when they were come into the house, they saw the young child with Mary his mother, and fell down, and worshipped him: and when

Adoration of the Magi, Ethiopia, 19th century

they had opened their treasures, they presented unto him gifts; gold, and frankincense, and myrrh.

2:12 And being warned of God in a dream that they should not return to Herod, they departed into their own country another way.

The Presentation of Jesus at the Temple, Fra Angelico, 1440–1441

The Presentation of Jesus in the Temple

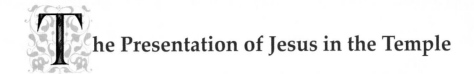

Luke

2:22 And when the days of her purification according to the law of Moses were accomplished, they brought him to Jerusalem, to present him to the Lord....

2:25 And, behold, there was a man in Jerusalem, whose name was Simeon; and the same man was just and devout ... and the Holy Ghost [*Spirit*] was upon him.

2:26 And it was revealed unto him by the Holy Ghost [*Spirit*], that he should not see death, before he had seen the Lord's Christ.

2:27 And he came by the Spirit into the temple: and when the parents brought in the child Jesus, to do for him after the custom of the law,

2:28 Then took he him up in his arms, and blessed God, and said,

2:29 "Lord, now lettest thou thy servant depart in peace, according to thy word:

The Presentation in the Temple, Fra Angelico, 1440–1441

2:30 For mine eyes have seen thy salvation,

2:31 Which thou hast prepared before the face of all people;

2:32 A light to lighten the Gentiles, and the glory of thy people Israel."

2:33 And Joseph and his mother marveled at those things which were spoken of him.

2:34 And Simeon blessed them, and said unto Mary his mother, "Behold, this child is set for the fall and rising again of many in Israel; and for a sign which shall be spoken against;

2:35 (Yea, a sword shall pierce through thy own soul also,) that the thoughts of many hearts may be revealed."

The Presentation of Christ, stained glass at Canterbury Cathedral, 12th century

The Presentation in the Temple, Cretan School, 17th century

The Flight into Egypt

Matthew

2:13 And when they were departed, behold, the angel of the Lord appeareth to Joseph in a dream, saying, "Arise, and take the young child and his mother, and flee into Egypt, and be thou there until I bring thee word: for Herod will seek the young child to destroy him."

2:14 When he arose, he took the young child and his mother by night, and departed into Egypt:

2:15 And was there until the death of Herod: that it might be fulfilled which was spoken of the Lord by the prophet, saying, "Out of Egypt have I called my son."

The Flight into Egypt,
Catherine Schuon, 1971

ⲆⲒⲘⲞⲨϮⲈⲠⲀⲨⲎⲢⲒ ⲈⲂⲞⲖ ϦⲈⲚⲬⲎⲘⲒ

2:16 Then Herod, when he saw that he was mocked of the wise men, was exceeding wroth [*angry*], and sent forth, and slew all the [*male*] children that were in Bethlehem, and in all the coasts thereof, from two years old and under, according to the time which he had diligently inquired of the wise men.

2:17 Then was fulfilled that which was spoken by Jeremiah the prophet, saying,

2:18 "In Rama was there a voice heard, lamentation, and weeping, and great mourning, Rachel weeping for her children, and would not be comforted, because they are not."

Opposite and above: Flight to Egypt, Coptic paintings, mid 20th century

Flight to Egypt, Fra Angelico, 1451–1452

2:19 But when Herod was dead, behold, an angel of the Lord appeareth in a dream to Joseph in Egypt,

2:20 Saying, "Arise, and take the young child and his mother, and go into the land of Israel: for they are dead which sought the young child's life."

2:21 And he arose, and took the young child and his mother, and came into the land of Israel....

2:23 And he came and dwelt in a city called Nazareth: that it might be fulfilled which was spoken by the prophets, "He shall be called a Nazarene."

Flight to Egypt, Bible from North Spain, 13th century

Part II:

The Childhood of Christ

There are several legends about the childhood of Christ that date to the first centuries of Christianity, but there is only one Biblical description of his youth.

The Boy Jesus with St. Joseph, altarpiece in the Church of the Holy Rosary, Rome

Christ Among the Doctors, Fra Angelico, 1438–1445

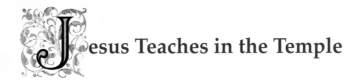esus Teaches in the Temple

Luke

2:40 And the child grew, and waxed strong in spirit, filled with wisdom: and the grace of God was upon him.

2:41 Now his parents went to Jerusalem every year at the feast of the passover.

2:42 And when he was twelve years old, they went up to Jerusalem after the custom of the feast.

2:43 And when they had fulfilled the days, as they returned, the child Jesus tarried [*remained*] behind in Jerusalem; and Joseph and his mother knew not of it.

Christ Among the Doctors, stained glass at Canterbury Cathedral, 12th century

Christ Among the Angels, Icon at the Monastery Dionysiu on Mount Athos, 17th century

2:44 But they, supposing him to have been in the company, went a day's journey; and they sought him among their kinsfolk and acquaintance.

2:45 And when they found him not, they turned back again to Jerusalem, seeking him.

2:46 And it came to pass, that after three days they found him in the temple, sitting in the midst of the doctors, both hearing them, and asking them questions.

2:47 And all that heard him were astonished at his understanding and answers.

2:48 And when they saw him, they were amazed: and his mother said unto him, "Son, why hast thou thus dealt with us? behold, thy father and I have sought thee sorrowing."

2:49 And he said unto them, "How is it that ye sought me? wist [*know*] ye not that I must be about my Father's business?"

2:50 And they understood not the saying which he spake unto them.

2:51 And he went down with them, and came to Nazareth, and was subject unto them: but his mother kept all these sayings in her heart.

2:52 And Jesus increased in wisdom and stature, and in favor with God and man.

Jesus Among the Doctors, Duccio di Buoninsegna, c. 1310

Part III:

The Teachings of Christ

Christ's essential teachings include
The Sermon on the Mount, which is the first
time The Lord's Prayer was spoken.

Christ, Frithjof Schuon, c. 1970

Sermon on the Mount, Fra Angelico, 1436–1443

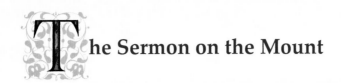

The Sermon on the Mount

Matthew

4:23 And Jesus went about all Galilee, teaching in their synagogues, and preaching the gospel of the kingdom, and healing all manner of sickness and all manner of disease among the people.

4:24 And his fame went throughout all Syria: and they brought unto him all sick people that were taken with divers diseases and torments, and those which were possessed with devils, and those which were lunatic, and those that had the palsy; and he healed them.

4:25 And there followed him great multitudes of people from Galilee, and from Decapolis, and from Jerusalem, and from Judaea, and from beyond the Jordan.

5:1 And seeing the multitudes, he went up into a mountain: and when he was set, his disciples came unto him:

5:2 And he opened his mouth, and taught them, saying,

The Beatitudes

5:3 "Blessed are the poor in spirit: for theirs is the kingdom of heaven.

5:4 Blessed are they that mourn: for they shall be comforted.

5:5 Blessed are the meek: for they shall inherit the earth.

5:6 Blessed are they which do hunger and thirst after righteousness: for they shall be filled.

5:7 Blessed are the merciful: for they shall obtain mercy.

5:8 Blessed are the pure in heart: for they shall see God.

5:9 Blessed are the peacemakers: for they shall be called the children of God.

5:10 Blessed are they which are persecuted for righteousness' sake: for theirs is the kingdom of heaven.

5:11 Blessed are ye, when men shall revile you, and persecute you, and shall say all manner of evil against you falsely, for my sake.

5:12 Rejoice, and be exceeding glad: for great is your reward in heaven: for so persecuted they the prophets which were before you.

The Salt of the Earth

5:13 Ye are the salt of the earth: but if the salt have lost his savor, wherewith shall it be salted? It is thenceforth good for nothing, but to be cast out, and to be trodden under foot of men.

The Light of the World

5:14 Ye are the light of the world. A city that is set on a hill cannot be hid.

5:15 Neither do men light a candle, and put it under a bushel, but on a candlestick; and it giveth light unto all that are in the house.

5:16 Let your light so shine before men, that they may see your good works, and glorify your Father which is in heaven.

Jesus' Attitude toward the Law

5:17 Think not that I am come to destroy the law, or the prophets: I am not come to destroy, but to fulfil.

5:18 For verily I say unto you, Till heaven and earth pass, one jot [*letter*] or one tittle [*stroke*] shall in no wise pass from the law, till all be fulfilled.

5:19 Whosoever therefore shall break one of these least commandments, and shall teach men so, he shall be called the least in the kingdom of heaven; but whosoever shall do and teach them, the same shall be called great in the kingdom of heaven.

5:20 For I say unto you, That except your righteousness shall exceed the righteousness of the scribes and Pharisees, ye shall in no case enter into the kingdom of heaven.

Jesus' Attitude toward Anger

5:21 Ye have heard that it was said of them of old time, 'Thou shalt not kill'; and 'whosoever shall kill shall be in danger of the judgment':

5:22 But I say unto you, That whosoever is angry with his brother without a cause shall be in danger of the judgment: and whosoever shall say to his brother, 'Raca' ['*worthless*'], shall be in danger of the council: but whosoever shall say, 'Thou fool,' shall be in danger of hell fire.

5:23 Therefore if thou bring thy gift to the altar, and there rememberest that thy brother hath ought against thee;

5:24 Leave there thy gift before the altar, and go thy way; first be reconciled to thy brother, and then come and offer thy gift.

5:25 Agree with thine adversary quickly, while thou art in the way with him; lest at any time the adversary deliver thee to the judge, and the judge deliver thee to the officer, and thou be cast into prison.

5:26 Verily I say unto thee, Thou shalt by no means come out thence, till thou hast paid the uttermost farthing [*last cent*].

Mosaic of Christ in the Garden of Gethsemane, Sant'Apollinare Nuovo, Ravenna, c. 500–520

Wedding at Cana, Catherine Schuon, 1975

Jesus' Attitude toward Adultery

5:27 Ye have heard that it was said by them of old time, 'Thou shalt not commit adultery':

5:28 But I say unto you, That whosoever looketh on a woman to lust after her hath committed adultery with her already in his heart.

5:29 And if thy right eye offend thee, pluck it out, and cast it from thee: for it is profitable for thee that one of thy members should perish, and not that thy whole body should be cast into hell.

5:30 And if thy right hand offend thee, cut it off, and cast it from thee: for it is profitable for thee that one of thy members should perish, and not that thy whole body should be cast into hell.

Jesus' Attitude toward Divorce

5:31 It hath been said, 'Whosoever shall put away his wife, let him give her a writing of divorcement':

5:32 But I say unto you, That whosoever shall put away his wife, saving for the cause of fornication, causeth her to commit adultery: and whosoever shall marry her that is divorced committeth adultery.

Jesus' Attitude toward Oaths

5:33 Again, ye have heard that it hath been said by them of old time, 'Thou shalt not forswear thyself [*swear falsely*], but shalt perform unto the Lord thine oaths':

5:34 But I say unto you, Swear not at all; neither by heaven; for it is God's throne:

5:35 Nor by the earth; for it is his footstool; neither by Jerusalem; for it is the city of the great King.

5:36 Neither shalt thou swear by thy head, because thou canst not make one hair white or black.

5:37 But let your communication be, 'Yea, yea; Nay, nay': for whatsoever is more than these cometh of evil.

Love for Enemies

5:38 Ye have heard that it hath been said, 'An eye for an eye, and a tooth for a tooth':

5:39 But I say unto you, That ye resist not evil: but whosoever shall smite [*strike*] thee on thy right cheek, turn to him the other also.

5:40 And if any man will sue thee at the law, and take away thy coat, let him have thy cloak also.

5:41 And whosoever shall compel thee to go a mile, go with him twain [*two*].

5:42 Give to him that asketh thee, and from him that would borrow of thee turn not thou away.

5:43 Ye have heard that it hath been said, 'Thou shalt love thy neighbor, and hate thine enemy.'

5:44 But I say unto you, Love your enemies, bless them that curse you, do good to them that hate you, and pray for them which despitefully use you, and persecute you;

5:45 That ye may be the children of your Father which is in heaven: for he maketh his sun to rise on the evil and on the good, and sendeth rain on the just and on the unjust.

5:46 For if ye love them which love you, what reward have ye? do not even the publicans [*tax collectors*] the same?

5:47 And if ye salute your brethren only, what do ye more than others? do not even the publicans [*tax collectors*] so?

5:48 Be ye therefore perfect, even as your Father which is in heaven is perfect.

Jesus' Teaching on Almsgiving

6:1 Take heed that ye do not your alms before men to be seen of [*by*] them: otherwise ye have no reward of your Father which is in heaven.

6:2 Therefore when thou doest thine alms, do not sound a trumpet before thee, as the hypocrites do in the synagogues and in the streets, that they may have glory of men. Verily I say unto you, They have their reward.

6:3 But when thou doest alms, let not thy left hand know what thy right hand doeth:

6:4 That thine alms may be in secret: and thy Father which seeth in secret himself shall reward thee openly.

Jesus' Teaching on Prayer

6:5 And when thou prayest, thou shalt not be as the hypocrites are: for they love to pray standing in the synagogues and in the corners of the

Christ Teaching, illumination from the Queen Mary Psalter, England, 14th century

Christ preaching, Chartres Cathedral, France, 13th century

streets, that they may be seen of men. Verily I say unto you, They have their reward.

6:6 But thou, when thou prayest, enter into thy closet, and when thou hast shut thy door, pray to thy Father which is in secret; and thy Father which seeth in secret shall reward thee openly.

6:7 But when ye pray, use not vain repetitions, as the heathen do: for they think that they shall be heard for their much speaking.

6:8 Be not ye therefore like unto them: for your Father knoweth what things ye have need of, before ye ask him.

6:9 After this manner therefore pray ye: Our Father which art in heaven, Hallowed be thy name.

6:10 Thy kingdom come, Thy will be done in earth, as it is in heaven.

6:11 Give us this day our daily bread.

6:12 And forgive us our debts, as we forgive our debtors.

6:13 And lead us not into temptation, but deliver us from evil: For thine is the kingdom, and the power, and the glory, for ever. Amen.

6:14 For if ye forgive men their trespasses, your heavenly Father will also forgive you:

6:15 But if ye forgive not men their trespasses, neither will your Father forgive your trespasses.

Jesus' Teaching on Fasting

6:16 Moreover when ye fast, be not, as the hypocrites, of a sad countenance: for they disfigure their faces, that they may appear unto men to fast. Verily I say unto you, They have their reward.

6:17 But thou, when thou fastest, anoint thine head, and wash thy face;

6:18 That thou appear not unto men to fast, but unto thy Father which is in secret: and thy Father, which seeth in secret, shall reward thee openly.

Treasure in Heaven

6:19 Lay not up for yourselves treasures upon earth, where moth and rust doth corrupt, and where thieves break through and steal:

6:20 But lay up for yourselves treasures in heaven, where neither moth nor rust doth corrupt, and where thieves do not break through nor steal:

6:21 For where thy treasure is, there will your heart be also.

6:22 The light of the body is the eye: if therefore thine eye be single, thy whole body shall be full of light.

6:23 But if thine eye be evil, thy whole body shall be full of darkness. If therefore the light that is in thee be darkness, how great is that darkness!

God and Mammon [riches]

6:24 No man can serve two masters; for either he will hate the one, and love the other; or else he will hold to the one, and despise the other. Ye cannot serve God and mammon [riches].

Care and Anxiety

6:25 Therefore I say unto you, Take no thought for your life, what ye shall eat, or what ye shall drink; nor yet for your body, what ye shall put on. Is not the life more than meat, and the body than raiment [clothing]?

6:26 Behold the fowls [birds] of the air: for they sow not, neither do they reap, nor gather into barns; yet your heavenly Father feedeth them. Are ye not much better than they?

6:27 Which of you by taking thought can add one cubit unto his stature?

6:28 And why take ye thought for raiment [clothing]? Consider the lilies of the field, how they grow; they toil not, neither do they spin:

6:29 And yet I say unto you, That even Solomon in all his glory was not arrayed like one of these.

6:30 Wherefore, if God so clothe the grass of the field, which to day is, and to morrow is cast into the oven, shall he not much more clothe you, O ye of little faith?

6:31 Therefore take no thought, saying, 'What shall we eat?' or, 'What shall we drink?' or, 'Wherewithal shall we be clothed?'

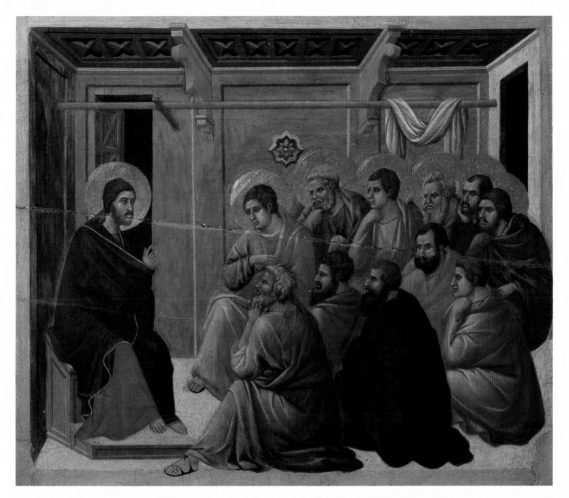

Christ Taking Leave of His Apostles, Duccio di Buoninsegna, 1308–1311

6:32 (For after all these things do the Gentiles seek:) for your heavenly Father knoweth that ye have need of all these things.

6:33 But seek ye first the kingdom of God, and his righteousness; and all these things shall be added unto you.

6:34 Take therefore no thought for the morrow: for the morrow shall take thought for the things of itself. Sufficient unto the day is the evil thereof.

Judging Others

7:1 Judge not, that ye be not judged.

7:2 For with what judgment ye judge, ye shall be judged: and with what measure ye mete, it shall be measured to you again.

7:3 And why beholdest thou the mote [*speck*] that is in thy brother's eye, but considerest not the beam that is in thine own eye?

7:4 Or how wilt thou say to thy brother, 'Let me pull the mote [*speck*] out of thine eye'; when, behold, a beam is in thine own eye?

7:5 Thou hypocrite, first cast out the beam out of thine own eye; and then shalt thou see clearly to cast out the mote [*speck*] out of thy brother's eye.

7:6 Give not that which is holy unto the dogs, neither cast ye your pearls before swine, lest they trample them under their feet, and turn again and rend [*tear*] you.

Ask, Seek, Knock

7:7 Ask, and it shall be given you; seek, and ye shall find; knock, and it shall be opened unto you:

7:8 For every one that asketh receiveth; and he that seeketh findeth; and to him that knocketh it shall be opened.

Christ Teaching the Lord's Prayer, medieval illumination, France, 12th century

7:9 Or what man is there of you, whom if his son shall ask bread, will he give him a stone?

7:10 Or if he ask for a fish, will he give him a serpent?

7:11 If ye then, being evil, know how to give good gifts unto your children, how much more shall your Father which is in heaven give good things to them that ask him?

7:12 Therefore all things whatsoever ye would that men should do to you, do ye even so to them: for this is the law and the prophets.

The Narrow Gate

7:13 Enter ye in at the strait gate: for wide is the gate, and broad is the way, that leadeth to destruction, and many there be which go in thereat.

7:14 Because strait is the gate, and narrow is the way, which leadeth unto life, and few there be that find it.

A Tree Is Known by Its Fruit

7:15 Beware of false prophets, which come to you in sheep's clothing, but inwardly they are ravening [*ravenous*] wolves.

7:16 Ye shall know them by their fruits. Do men gather grapes of thorns, or figs of thistles?

7:17 Even so every good tree bringeth forth good fruit; but a corrupt tree bringeth forth evil fruit.

7:18 A good tree cannot bring forth evil fruit, neither can a corrupt tree bring forth good fruit.

7:19 Every tree that bringeth not forth good fruit is hewn down, and cast into the fire.

7:20 Wherefore by their fruits ye shall know them.

I Never Knew You

7:21 Not every one that saith unto me, 'Lord, Lord,' shall enter into the kingdom of heaven; but he that doeth the will of my Father which is in heaven.

7:22 Many will say to me in that day, 'Lord, Lord, have we not prophesied in thy name? and in thy name have cast out devils? and in thy name done many wonderful works?'

7:23 And then will I profess [*declare*] unto them, 'I never knew you: depart from me, ye that work iniquity.'

The Two Foundations

7:24 Therefore whosoever heareth these sayings of mine, and doeth them, I will liken him unto a wise man, which built his house upon a rock:

7:25 And the rain descended, and the floods came, and the winds blew, and beat upon that house; and it fell not: for it was founded upon a rock.

7:26 And every one that heareth these sayings of mine, and doeth them not, shall be likened unto a foolish man, which built his house upon the sand:

7:27 And the rain descended, and the floods came, and the winds blew, and beat upon that house; and it fell: and great was the fall of it."

7:28 And it came to pass, when Jesus had ended these sayings, the people were astonished at his doctrine:

7:29 For he taught them as one having authority, and not as the scribes.

The Transfiguration, Fra Angelico, 1437–1446

Illustrations

Frontispiece: *The Virgin of the Sleigh*, Catherine Schuon, 1969.

Title page: *Adoration of the Magi*, Fra Angelico, 1423–1424.

p. *viii*: *Annunciation and Adoration of the Magi*, Fra Angelico, before 1434. Museo di San Marco, Florence.

p. 1: *The Madonna of Humility*, Lippo di Dalmasio, c. 1390. The National Gallery, London.

p. 2: *St. John the Baptist: Angel of the Desert*, Procopius Chirin, 7th century. Tretyakov Gallery, Moscow.

p. 4: *The Naming of John*, Fra Angelico, c. 1434–1435. Museo di San Marco, Florence.

pp. 6–7: *The Annunciation*, Catherine Schuon, 1967.

p. 8: *The Annunciation*, Catherine Schuon, 1967.

p. 10: *The Annunciation*. Icon from the Peribleptos Church (Saint Clement), early 14th century. National Museum, Ohrid, Macedonia.

p. 11: *The Annunciation*, Fra Angelico, c. 1441. Cell 3, Museo di San Marco, Florence.

pp. 12–13: *The Visitation*, Catherine Schuon, 1970.

p. 14: *The Visitation* (detail), Giotto, 1302–1305. Fresco in the Capella degli Scrovegni, Padua, Italy.

p. 15: *The Visitation* (detail), Fra Angelico, c. 1432–1434. Museo Diocesano, Cortona, Italy.

p. 16: *The Magnificat*, Catherine Schuon, 1969.

p. 18: *Angels*. Detail from a painting by Catherine Schuon, 1971.

p. 19: *The Angel Tells Joseph to Flee to Egypt*. Ceiling painting in the Church of St. Martin in Zillis, Switzerland, 1130.

p. 20: *The Nativity*, Alesso Baldovinetti, Fra Angelico, and assistants, c. 1441. The Armadio degli Argenti, Santissima Annunziata, Florence. Cell 5, Museo di San Marco, Florence.

p. 21: *The Nativity*. Medieval painting, c. 1200.

p. 22: *The Annunciation to the Shepherds*, School of Reichenau, early 11th century. Illumination to the *Book of Pericopes of Henry II*. Bayerische Staatsbibliothek, Munich.

p. 23: *The Annunciation to the Shepherds*. Ceiling painting in the Church of St. Martin in Zillis, Switzerland, 1130.

p. 23: *The Annunciation to the Shepherds*, Giotto, c. 1310. Fresco on the Lower Church, Basilica of Assisi.

p. 24: *The Nativity*. Medieval illumination, France, 15th century.

p. 25: *The Virgin of the Rose Garden*, Stefan Lochner, c. 1448. Wallraf-Richartz Museum, Cologne.

p. 26: *The Nativity*, Lou Houng-Nie. China, early 20th century.

p. 27: *The Virgin and the Child*, Lou Houng-Nie. China, early 20th century.

p. 28: *The Adoration of the Magi*, Catherine Schuon, 1968.

pp. 30–31: *The Adoration of the Magi*, Ethiopia, 19th century. Private collection, Paris.

p. 32: *The Presentation of Jesus at the Temple*, Fra Angelico, 1440–1441. Cell 10, Museo di San Marco, Florence.

p. 33: *The Presentation in the Temple* (detail), Fra Angelico, c. 1432–1434. Museo Diocesano, Cortona, Italy.

p. 34: *The Presentation of Christ*. Stained glass at Canterbury Cathedral, England, 12th century.

p. 35: *The Presentation in the Temple*, Cretan School, 17th century. Russian Museum, Saint Petersburg.

pp. 36–37: *The Flight into Egypt*, Catherine Schuon, 1971.

p. 38: *Flight to Egypt*. Coptic painting, mid 20th century.

Biographical Notes

CATHERINE SCHUON was born in Bern, Switzerland, in 1924 and is a gifted artist and translator, fluent in English, German, French, and Spanish; nine of her paintings are included in this volume. She has collected children's books her entire life and is dedicated to helping children appreciate the beauty of the world's religions, which has inspired her to co-edit this book.

As the daughter of a career Swiss diplomat she spent her youth in Europe, North Africa, and South America, excelling at languages and painting. In May 1949, she married author Frithjof Schuon and began translating his correspondence into English and Spanish. Catherine later edited a volume on art from her husband's writings titled *Art from the Sacred to the Profane: East and West*. In 1980, the Schuons moved from Lake Geneva to southern Indiana, where Catherine still lives to this day.

MICHAEL OREN FITZGERALD is the author and editor of over a dozen books that have received more than two dozen awards, including the prestigious ForeWord Book of the Year Award, the Ben Franklin Award, and the USA Best Books Award. Fitzgerald's award-winning books include *Christian Spirit, Foundations of Christian Art* by Titus Burckhardt, and *Sermon of All Creation: Christians on Nature*. His books have been published in six different languages and at least ten of his books and two documentary films produced by him are used in university classes.

Michael and his wife, award-winning editor Judith Fitzgerald, live outside Bloomington, Indiana and spend their time surrounded by their children and grandchildren, who are at the root of their desire to produce quality books for children and young adults.

Other Titles on Christianity by Wisdom Tales and World Wisdom

Chartres and the Birth of the Cathedral: Revised,
by Titus Burckhardt, 2010

A Christian Pilgrim in India:
The Spiritual Journey of Swami Abhishiktananda (Henri Le Saux),
by Harry Oldmeadow, 2008

Christian Spirit,
edited by Judith Fitzgerald and Michael Oren Fitzgerald, 2004

A Christian Woman's Secret: A Modern-Day Journey to God,
by Lilian Staveley, 2009

Christianity/Islam: Perspectives on Esoteric Ecumenism
A New Translation with Selected Letters,
by Frithjof Schuon, 2008

The Destruction of the Christian Tradition: Updated and Revised,
by Rama P. Coomaraswamy, 2006

For God's Greater Glory: Gems of Jesuit Spirituality,
edited by Jean-Pierre Lafouge, 2006

The Foundations of Christian Art: Illustrated,
by Titus Burckhardt, 2006

The Fullness of God: Frithjof Schuon on Christianity,
selected and edited by James S. Cutsinger, 2004

In the Heart of the Desert, Revised:
The Spirituality of the Desert Fathers and Mothers,
by John Chryssavgis, 2008

Messenger of the Heart:
The Book of Angelus Silesius,
translated, introduced, and drawn by Frederick Franck, 2005